CIVICS
Q & A

WHAT ARE CHECKS AND BALANCES?

Leslie Harper

PowerKiDS
press.
New York

Published in 2013 by The Rosen Publishing Group, Inc.
29 East 21st Street, New York, NY 10010

First Edition

Editor: Jennifer Way
Book Design: Ashley Drago
Layout Design: Andrew Povolny

Photo Credits: Cover, p. 21 MCT/Contributor/Getty Images; p. 4 iStockphoto/Thinkstock; p. 5 (top) Cristina Ciochina/Shutterstock.com; p. 5 (bottom) Vacclav/Shutterstock.com; p. 6 MPI/Stringer/Archive Photos/Getty Images; p. 9 (top) Bill Clark/CQ-Roll Call Group/Getty Images; pp. 9, 18 (bottom) Bloomberg/Contributor/Getty Images; p. 10 Saul Loeb/AFP/Getty Images; p. 13 Kansas City Star/McClatchy-Tribune/Getty Images; p. 14 George Bridges/AFP/Getty Images; p. 17 Tim Sloan/AFP/Getty Images.

Library of Congress Cataloging-in-Publication Data

Harper, Leslie.
 What are checks and balances? / by Leslie Harper. — 1st ed.
    p. cm. — (Civics Q&A)
 Includes index.
 ISBN 978-1-4488-7433-0 (library binding) — ISBN 978-1-4488-7506-1 (pbk.) —
ISBN 978-1-4488-7580-1 (6-pack)
1. Separation of powers—United States–Juvenile literature. 2. United States—Politics and government —
Juvenile literature. I. Title.
 JK305.H38 2013
 320.473'04—dc23
                                    2011051869

Manufactured in the United States of America

CPSIA Compliance Information: Batch #SW12PK: For Further Information contact Rosen Publishing, New York, New York at 1-800-237-9932

CONTENTS

WHAT ARE CHECKS AND BALANCES?

In some forms of government, one person can become very powerful. In the United States, though, the government is divided into three branches, or groups. These branches are called the **legislative** branch, the **executive** branch, and the **judicial** branch. The three branches each have different roles, or jobs.

The Supreme Court Building is where the Supreme Court meets. It is the head of the judicial branch.

4

The US government uses a system of **checks and balances**. This means that each branch of the government can check, or control, some parts of what the other branches do. This creates a balance of power in which no one person or group can become too powerful.

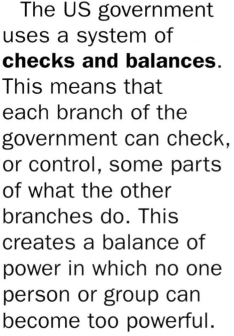

The US Capitol is where Congress meets. Congress is the legislative branch. It is made up of the Senate and the House of Representatives.

The White House is where the president lives. The president is head of the executive branch.

WHAT IS THE CONSTITUTION?

The Framers met in Philadelphia, Pennsylvania, in the summer of 1787 to write the Constitution.

The US Constitution is the highest law in the United States. It was written in 1787. The men who wrote it are often called the Framers. This is because the Constitution set up a frame, or structure, for how the new government of the United States would work.

The Framers wanted power to be shared in their new country. To do this, they created the three branches of government. In the Constitution, the Framers created a way for all parts of the government to work together.

US Constitution

WHAT IS THE LEGISLATIVE BRANCH?

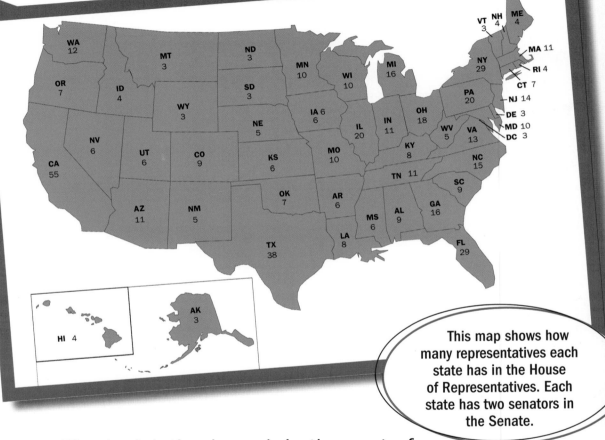

| WA 12 | MT 3 | ND 3 | MN 10 | WI 10 | MI 16 | | | | VT 3 | NH 4 | ME 4 |

Map labels:
WA 12, MT 3, ND 3, MN 10, WI 10, MI 16, VT 3, NH 4, ME 4, NY 29, MA 11, RI 4, OR 7, ID 4, SD 3, PA 20, CT 7, NJ 14, WY 3, IA 6, IN 11, OH 18, DE 3, MD 10, DC 3, NV 6, NE 5, IL 20, WV 5, VA 13, CA 55, UT 6, CO 9, KS 6, MO 10, KY 8, NC 15, TN 11, SC 9, AZ 11, NM 5, OK 7, AR 6, AL 9, GA 16, MS 6, LA 8, FL 29, TX 38, AK 3, HI 4

This map shows how many representatives each state has in the House of Representatives. Each state has two senators in the Senate.

The legislative branch is the part of the government that makes laws. It is made up of two groups, called the Senate and the House of Representatives. Together, these two groups are called **Congress**. Members of the US Congress

8

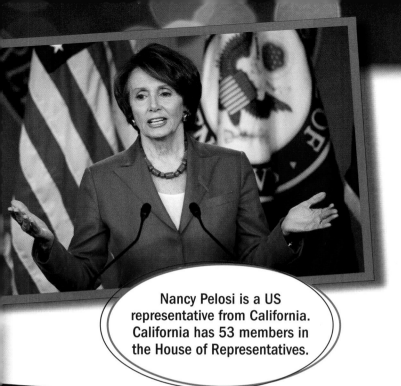

Nancy Pelosi is a US representative from California. California has 53 members in the House of Representatives.

write laws and vote on which laws will take effect. They also have the power to print money and can vote to go to war with another country.

Each state government has its own legislative branch, too. A state's congress makes laws that apply only in that state. The US Congress makes laws that apply to the whole country.

Olympia Snowe is a senator from Maine. Each state has two senators in the US Senate.

HOW IS THE LEGISLATIVE BRANCH LIMITED?

The president can either veto or approve the laws passed by the legislative branch. Here is President Obama signing a piece of legislation.

The power to write laws makes the legislative branch a very important part of the government. However, the executive branch and the judicial branch limit its power somewhat. When Congress has voted to pass a new law, that law must be approved or **vetoed** by the president, who

is a member of the executive branch. Sometimes a person or group believes that one of Congress's laws is **unconstitutional**, or goes against the US Constitution. People can ask the **Supreme Court**, the head of the judicial branch, to look at the law and decide whether or not it is unconstitutional.

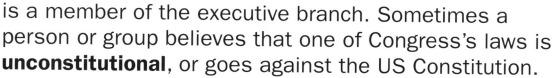

This diagram shows how the executive and judicial branches limit the powers of the legislative branch.

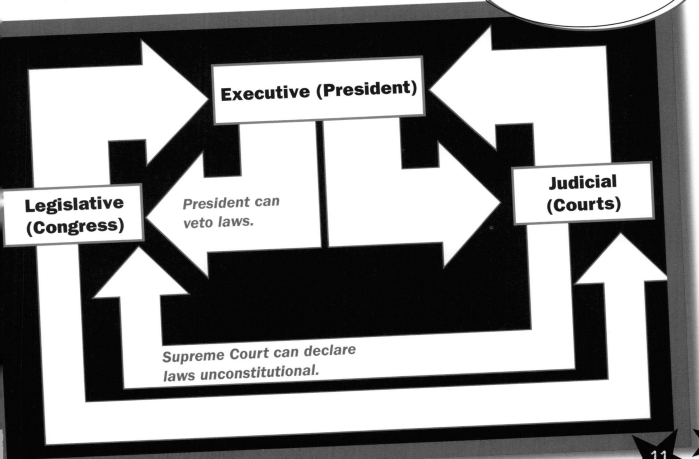

Executive (President)

Legislative (Congress)

Judicial (Courts)

President can veto laws.

Supreme Court can declare laws unconstitutional.

WHAT IS THE EXECUTIVE BRANCH?

The role of the executive branch is to make sure that laws are executed, or carried out. The president leads the executive branch. He can approve or veto laws written by Congress and meet with the leaders of other countries. He also nominates, or suggests, people to serve on the Supreme Court and in other important positions.

The vice president helps the president perform these duties. The executive branch also includes many departments concerned with issues such as education, energy, and housing. The heads of these departments are members of the president's **cabinet**. They meet with the president and give their advice.

The president is the leader of the executive branch. Barack Obama is the forty-fourth president of the United States.

13

HOW IS THE EXECUTIVE BRANCH LIMITED?

The House of Representatives has impeached only two presidents. They are Andrew Johnson and Bill Clinton (center). The Senate cleared both presidents.

The president can do little without working with the other two branches. The Senate, part of the legislative branch, must approve anyone whom the president nominates to serve on the Supreme Court or as the head of a department. Congress must also approve agreements that the president makes with other countries. The legislative branch may **impeach** the president if he commits a crime while in office.

One of the president's most important jobs is as the leader of the US military. This means he has the power to command troops. However, only Congress can declare war.

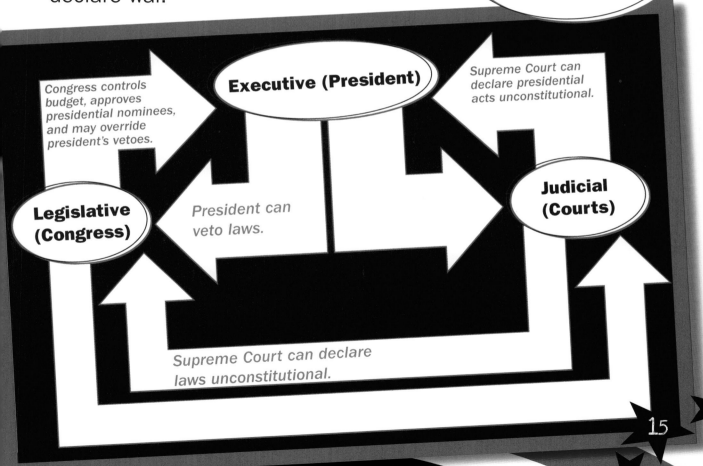

This diagram shows how the legislative and judicial branches limit the powers of the executive branch.

Executive (President)

Congress controls budget, approves presidential nominees, and may override president's vetoes.

Supreme Court can declare presidential acts unconstitutional.

Legislative (Congress)

President can veto laws.

Judicial (Courts)

Supreme Court can declare laws unconstitutional.

WHAT IS THE JUDICIAL BRANCH?

The judicial branch of the government is made up of the US court system. Its job is to interpret, or understand and explain, the laws of the country. The highest court in the United States is the Supreme Court. It is made up of eight judges and a chief **justice**.

When a person or group feels that a lower court has made a mistake or that a law is unconstitutional, those people can ask the Supreme Court to hear their case. The Supreme Court will listen to arguments and then decide what a law means and whether it goes against the Constitution.

There are nine justices in the Supreme Court, shown here. Their rulings on cases are decided by a majority. That means at least five justices must agree on a ruling.

HOW IS THE JUDICIAL BRANCH LIMITED?

Here is Sonia Sotomayor at her confirmation hearing. After the Senate approved President Obama's nomination of her, Sotomayor joined the Supreme Court.

Supreme Court justices serve until they decide to step down. The writers of the Constitution created the court this way so that, unlike the president and members of Congress, the justices could make hard decisions without having to worry about being **elected**.

The judicial branch is still limited by the other two branches, though. The president nominates people to become Supreme Court justices. The Senate must then approve those nominations. If a justice commits a serious crime, she can be impeached by a vote in Congress.

This diagram shows how the legislative and executive branches limit the powers of the judicial branch.

Executive (President)

Congress controls budget, approves presidential nominees, and may override president's vetoes.

Supreme Court can declare presidential acts unconstitutional

Legislative (Congress)

President can veto laws.

Nominates justices.

Judicial (Courts)

Supreme Court can declare laws unconstitutional.

Approves president's nominations and can impeach judges.

A BALANCE OF POWER

What do you think would happen if one person in the government held all the power? You likely would not agree with all of that person's choices. The Framers of the Constitution worked hard to create a fair system of checks and balances. They wanted a government that would serve all people without allowing one person or group to become too strong.

Keeping this balance of power is one of the most important ways that our government stays fair. Our government works best when all three branches share power and work together.

Sharing power between the three branches of government is not always easy. It is an important foundation of a fair government, though.

CHECKS AND BALANCES Q&A

1

Q: Can the Constitution ever be changed?

A: **Yes, changes to the Constitution are called amendments.**

2

Q: What is the Bill of Rights?

A: **The Bill of Rights is the first 10 amendments to the Constitution.**

3

Q: Who was the first woman to serve on the Supreme Court?

A: **Sandra Day O'Connor was the first woman to serve on the Supreme Court. She served from 1981 until 2006.**

4

Q: Have any US presidents been impeached?

A: **Andrew Johnson and Bill Clinton were impeached by the House of Representatives and tried in the Senate. Both were found not guilty, though, and stayed in office.**

5

Q: How many members of Congress are there?

A: **There are 435 members of the House of Representatives and 100 senators, for a total of 535 people who serve in Congress.**

6

Q: How do we decide how many representatives each state gets in Congress?

A: **Each state has two senators. The number of people each state sends to the House of Representatives is decided by how many people live in that state.**

GLOSSARY

cabinet (KAB-nit) A group of people who act as advisers to important government officials.

checks and balances (CHEKS UND BA-lunts-ez) A system in which the powers of government are separated into branches with no one branch having too much power.

Congress (KON-gres) The part of the US government that makes laws.

elected (ee-LEK-tid) Picked for an office by voters.

executive (eg-ZEK-yoo-tiv) Referring to the top branch of government, which includes the president.

impeach (im-PEECH) To remove from office because of misconduct.

judicial (joo-DIH-shul) Relating to the function or administration of the court system.

justice (JUS-tis) Another word for a judge.

legislative (LEH-jis-lay-tiv) Having to do with the branch of government that makes laws and collects taxes.

Supreme Court (suh-PREEM KORT) The highest court in the United States.

unconstitutional (un-kon-stih-TOO-shuh-nul) Having to do with going against the basic rules by which a country or a state is governed.

vetoed (VEE-tohd) Did not allow laws proposed by another branch of government to pass.

23

INDEX

WEBSITES

Due to the changing nature of Internet links, PowerKids Press has developed an online list of websites related to the subject of this book. This site is updated regularly. Please use this link to access the list: www.powerkidslinks.com/civ/check/